**Library of Congress Cataloging-in-Publication Data**
**Bombarde, Odile**
  Living in Ancient Rome/written by Odile Bombarde and Claude
Moatti; illustrated by François Place. Translation of: Comment
vivaient les Romains?
  Summary: Describes in text and illustrations, various aspects
of day-to-day life in ancient Rome.
  1. Rome — Social life and customs — Juvenile
literature.[1. Rome — Social life and customs.] I. Moatti,
Claude. II. Place, François, ill. III. Title. IV. Series: Young
Discovery Library (Series); 8.
DG78.B6613   1988            937—dc19            87-37113
ISBN 0-944589-08-1

Written by Odile Bombarde
and Claude Moatti
Illustrated by François Place

*Specialist Adviser:*
*François Hinard*
*Professor of Roman History*
*University of Caen*

*ISBN 0-944589-08-1*
*First U.S. Publication 1988 by*
*Young Discovery Library*
*217 Main St. · Ossining, NY 10562*

©*1986 by Editions Gallinard*
*Translated by Sarah Matthews*
*English text* ©*1987 by Moonlight Publishing Ltd.*
*Thanks to Aileen Buhl*

$4.95

YOUNG DISCOVERY LIBRARY

# Living in
# Ancient Rome

Some cities in the world
    are thousands of years old...

YOUNG DISCOVERY LIBRARY

# This city is nearly three-thousand years old!

It is Rome, the capital of Italy.
Today, in and around the busy streets, you can see old ruins, like the Coliseum, left over from long ago.
The streets of ancient Rome were once as busy and noisy as the streets of modern Rome are today.

# What was it like, living in Rome around the time Christ was born?

The Romans were governed by their Emperor Augustus and Roman power stretched over all the lands around the Mediterranean Sea. Everywhere, in the countries the Romans ruled, you can still find the remains of their buildings, roads, and everyday objects like pots and coins. They have left traces of their lives wherever they settled.

This Roman coin has a picture of Augustus, the first Roman Emperor.
(The writing says 'Augustus Divi F.': 'Augustus God's Son'.)

The Coliseum in Rome, as it looks today

# What a din!

During the night, you would hear the carts rumbling along the roads, and the drivers swearing at their animals. During

Roman scales

the day, crowds of people pushed and bustled past. There were so many people living in some parts of Rome that buildings were six or seven stories high. They often caught fire; the Romans set up one of the earliest fire companies. Packed with shops and monuments and all the business of government, Rome attracted people from all over the Empire — traders, teachers, philosophers and fighters.

In the taverns, the men would sit and drink wine.

Men would go to the barber's to be shaved and perfumed.

# How did a Roman spend his day?

The Roman here was very well off, and lived in a big house. At daybreak, he woke up and had a breakfast of bread and cheese, before giving out the day's money or food to the people he looked after. Slaves did all the housework. The main meal of the day, the **cena**, was in the middle of the afternoon. Often, a lot of friends would be invited to share it. They used to lie on couches, and eat with their fingers. What did they eat? Boiled ostrich, spiced porcupines, fried roses...Poorer Romans had simpler meals: bread, olives, grapes and honey. They ate very little meat.

As soon as it was dark, most people went to bed. The only lights were oil lamps, and they were smoky and expensive to run.

Every house had an altar, where offerings were left for the Lares, the household gods.

The mistress of the house had her hair done and her face made up every morning by slaves.

There weren't many Roman houses with bathrooms. Most people just washed in a bowl of water.

## How did the Romans dress?

The men wore togas, the women dresses caught up around the waist. Boys wore a locket, a bulla, at their necks as a protective charm.

1, 2. Slaves wearing tunics

3, 4. The master and mistress

The toga was semicircular and could be draped in different ways.

School was held in an alcove, shut off from the street by a curtain.

## Off to school

Only a few boys, between seven and fifteen years old, went to school. They would set off very early in the morning. A slave went with each boy to carry his wax tablets and the sharp stylus used to write on them. The teacher was often a foreigner, a Greek. He would punish bad pupils with a rod called a ferula.

## What games did Roman children play?

They had toys such as hoops, wooden tops, and dolls made of wax or of clay. They played at jacks...Sometimes they invented games with nuts, making them into little carriages to tie to mice.

What a schoolboy needed: papyrus rolls — these were the Roman books — pens and inkwell, a wax tablet, styli.

**This is the Forum, the main public meeting place in Rome.**
Most of the buildings here were made of white marble. Augustus added so many important buildings to Rome, in the Forum and elsewhere, that he said: "I found Rome brick and left it marble."

There were temples and triumphal arches, and inscriptions to remind Romans of their famous past and their responsibilities for the future.

2. Temple of Jupiter on the Capitol
2. Via Sacra, the 'sacred way' leading to the temples
3. Rostrums. Men stood up here to make speeches on the important issues of the day.
4. Record office, where all the public records were kept.

The baths had different pools, some hot, some warm, some cold.

Nearly every afternoon, all the well-off Roman men went to the public **baths.** They bathed there and talked with their friends and played games.

It was one of the great pleasures of their lives! The **water** which Rome needed was brought to the city by means of fourteen aqueducts. They carried it to the baths, to the gardens, to the public lavatories, and to the fountains. Water for the houses was fetched in big earthenware pots called **amphorae.**

The first Roman sewer was built 2,500 years ago and is still used today!

The Romans were great shipbuilders

# Rome was the marketplace for all the world.

Most things came by sea, in huge merchant ships. Wrecks have been found which had ten-thousand amphorae on board. These long clay pots held everything from wine to oil.

Carts weren't so good for carrying things. Whether they had two wheels or four, they were slow, bumpy and expensive to run.

A warehouse

A shop

**Ostia was the port of Rome.** As soon as a ship arrived there, its cargo was taken off and loaded onto a riverboat. These small boats traveled up the River Tiber to the warehouses in Rome, where the cargo was stored.

You could buy anything in Rome, because the whole of the Empire sent its produce there.

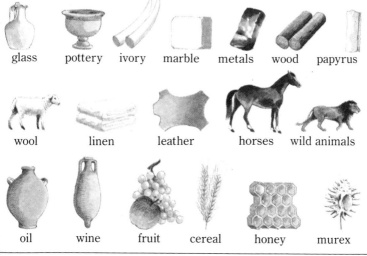

glass    pottery    ivory    marble    metals    wood    papyrus

wool    linen    leather    horses    wild animals

oil    wine    fruit    cereal    honey    murex

An olive oil press

The jars were kept cool, up to their necks in soil.

## In the Italian countryside, lots of people were hard at work.

There were slaves working for their masters, and small farmers working the land for themselves. They grew vines for grapes and wine, and harvested olives for olive oil.

Each big farm had its own flour mill and bakery.

The Romans used a lot of olive oil; they didn't make butter. They kept herds of goats and sheep. The soil was worked with a simple wooden plough which broke up the soil. It was pulled along by a pair of oxen. Sometimes, in between the vines and the cypress trees, there were beautiful houses, called **villas,** where rich Romans came to get away from the noise and bustle of the city.

Each chariot team had its own color and claimed the protection of a particular god: Jupiter for the whites, Neptune the blues, etc. They had their own fans, too, like modern football clubs.

## Bread and circuses!

That's what the Roman Emperors gave the people to keep them happy. Almost every other day there would be something to go and watch: chariot races, **gladiator** fights, plays...

The Romans liked gambling for money with dice.

All the shows were free.
Sometimes there might be a hundred
chariot races held in a single day.
These games were held on a racetrack
called the Circus Maximus, which the
chariots had to go around seven times (it
was called a circus because they went
around in a circle). Up to 250,000 people
could watch and bet on the chariots as
they hurtled along.

# Wild animals and men fought together in the amphitheatres.

The biggest amphitheatre of all was the Coliseum. Fifty-thousand people could sit all around it on the stone benches. In the center was a huge arena, with a barrier around the edge to protect the spectators from the wild animals. A canvas roof was stretched over the top in the middle of the day to protect people from the bright sunshine. The amphitheatre could be used for mock sea battles too; the whole arena was flooded, and real boats brought in to sail on the water.

Underneath the seats were passages along which the animals could be led into the arena, and where all the materials for the different shows could be stored.

## The games went on from sunrise to sundown.

Sometimes there were men hiding behind iron grills, firing arrows at the wild animals. At other times, gladiators fought the animals face-to-face, with just a spear or a sword against bulls, lions, panthers, tigers... There were animal fights, too: a bear against a bull, or an elephant against a rhinoceros. Perhaps cruelest of all was when the gladiators were made to fight each other. Some gladiators were popular professional fighters, others were slaves or condemned criminals, or poor people attracted by the chance of high wages.

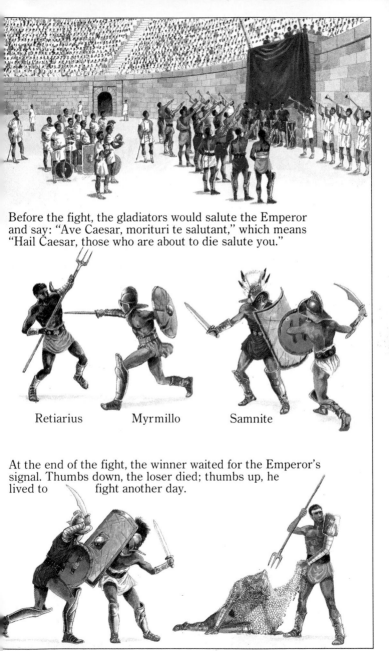

Before the fight, the gladiators would salute the Emperor
and say: "Ave Caesar, morituri te salutant," which means
"Hail Caesar, those who are about to die salute you."

Retiarius          Myrmillo          Samnite

At the end of the fight, the winner waited for the Emperor's
signal. Thumbs down, the loser died; thumbs up, he
lived to          fight another day.

At the back of the theater was a high wall. It was used for scenery and bounced the actors' voices back towards the audience.

**At the theater,** the public could watch comedies or tragedies. Most popular of all, though, were knockabout farces, mimes or pantomimes with music and songs. The first big stone theater was built at the time of Julius Caesar. If an audience got too noisy, the producer would call for silence: "Slaves must not sit all over the place; nurses must not bring babies with them, and women must laugh silently!"

Actors wore masks to show which characters they were playing. This is Dionysos, god of the theater.

A comic actor, shown in a mosaic

**For a long time, the games were held in honor of the gods.** Their gods were very important to the Romans. There were a lot of different ones, but the most important of them was the Father of the Gods, Jupiter. The Romans asked the gods for their protection and help through sacrifices of goats, pigs and bulls. The animals for sacrifice were decorated with garlands of flowers, and then led to the altar where the priest killed them with an axe.

Before a battle, the priest would watch the sacred hens to see how they behaved.
If they ate their grain hungrily, it was a good sign.

Have you seen remains of the Roman occupation during vacation, like Hadrian's Wall here or the triumphal arch below?

From Spain to Syria, from North Africa to the borders of Scotland, **the Roman army conquered a vast Empire.** The Romans had to set safe boundaries to their conquests. The soldiers built fortified camps everywhere, and constructed a huge network of roads so that the army could move about quickly. A lot of the roads still remain. They usually go straight from point to point.

◀ The soldiers have set up camp. Now they will build solid huts to live in.

## The Roman legion at war

There were 310,000 soldiers at the
time of Augustus. Half of them were
legionaries, well-armed foot soldiers,
the rest were cavalry and archers. Here
the army is besieging a town. The
soldiers have catapults (1) to throw
stones and arrows against the
defenders, a battering ram (2) to break
down the gate, and a siege tower (3)
and scaling ladders (4) so that they can
climb over the walls and into the town.

**The Romans triumphant** After a great victory, the Emperor was given a triumph: a procession through Rome.

3. Then followed the animals prepared for sacrifice, and the prisoners of war.

5. He wore special clothes: a purple tunic embroidered with gold, golden sandals, an ivory scepter and a crown of laurel leaves.

2. At the head of the procession came musicians, then porters carrying all the booty which had been won, and models of the towns which had been captured.

4. Finally, with officers and soldiers in front of him and behind him, came the triumphant Emperor in his chariot.

6. Behind him stood a slave holding over his head a golden crown taken from a statue of Jupiter. His children rode with him or on horseback behind.

## The Romans live on in our language.

They didn't leave only remains made of stone or metal, they left traces of their language too. Thousands of English words come from Latin, the language the Romans spoke. For example, there's the word 'example' itself, which comes from the Latin *exemplum.* And 'language' comes from the Latin *lingua.* A lot of English people call their house a *villa,* just as the Romans did. The 'pedal' on your bike comes from the Latin word for 'feet', *pedes* ('pedestrian' comes from the same word as well). A 'mile' is called that because it was a thousand (*mille*) paces for a Roman foot soldier. And 'computer' comes from the Latin word for 'to calculate', *computare.*

The Romans had a story that Rome was founded by Aeneas, a Trojan hero. You can see him here fleeing with his household from Troy after it has been burned by the Greeks.

Books of Discovery for children five through ten . . .

**Young Discovery Library** is an international undertaking — the series is now published in nine countries. It is the world's first pocket encyclopedia for children, 120 titles will be published.

Each title in the series is an education on the subject covered: a collaboration among the author, the illustrator, an advisory group of elementary school teachers and an academic specialist on the subject.

The goal is to respond to the endless curiousity of children, to fascinate and educate.